MESSIANIC SHABBAT SERVICE

A **BE KY** Book ©

By Hollisa Alewine, PhD

DEDICATION

To The Olive Branch, faithful friends.

CONTENTS

GLOSSARY

Adonai – my Lord

Amidah – the Standing Prayer prayed three times daily

aron – the cabinet that contains the Torah scroll or other scrolls

beit din – a rabbinic court that decides practical matters

bimah – the piece of furniture, usually elevated, on which the Torah scroll is unrolled for public reading

Brit HaChadasha – New Testament, or literally, "New Covenant"

chazzan – someone skilled in leading public prayer, which is usually sung; the person may also be called a cantor

El Shaddai – the all-sufficient God

gabbai – someone who helps with the administrative, orderly running of a synagogue service; this person is also sometimes called a shamash.

Haftorah – portion of Scripture from the Prophets that is read along with the customary portion of the Torah read in a particular week

halakha – the method of walking out the Scriptures according to Jewish law

hitpallel – to pray, in the reflexive sense of the verb, to judge one's self

kavanah – the passion and intention that is to accompany prayer

Ketuvim – the section of the TANAKH known as the Writings; it contains books such as the Psalms and the Book of Esther

Kiddush – a cup of wine that accompanies special celebrations, especially Shabbat meals

kippah – a cap worn by observant Jews

Mashiach – Messiah

megillah – a scroll, such as the scroll of Esther

mezuzah – a small container affixed to the doorpost of a Jewish home; it contains Scriptures written by a scribe, and it fulfills the commandment to write His words "on the doorposts of your house…"

midrash – reading, discussing, and teasing out the meaning and significance of the Scriptures

mikveh – a pool of living water for immersion, similar to the Christian baptistry

moedim – the Biblical feast days: Passover, Unleavened Bread, Firstfruits of the Barley, Pentecost, Feast of Trumpets, Day of Atonement, and Tabernacles

Ner Tamid – "always light": the light for the ark in a synagogue that always stays lit

Neviim – division of Scripture known as the Prophets

Oneg – pleasure or delight of the Shabbat; it is used to describe the meal and/or refreshments following a synagogue service

parokhet – the curtain or veil of the ark

seder – order; it can refer to an order of service, such as a Passover seder

shammash – servant; this office in the synagogue may be likened to a deacon

Shmonei Esrei – "18." The Shmonei Esrei is another name for the Amidah, the prayer prayed three times daily by observant Jews (see the BEKY Booklet *Standing With Israel: a House of Prayer for*

All Nations for a detailed explanation of the prayer's prophetic implications)

shofar – ram's horn used as a trumpet

siddur – a prayerbook

sofer – scribe

tallit or tallit katan – a rectangular garment to which fringes are affixed. The tallit is put on for prayer, but the tallit katan may be worn over or under the shirt throughout the day

TANAKH – Tanakh is an acronym for Torah, Neviim, Ketuvim, or Law, Prophets, and Writings, the ancient divisions of the Hebrew Bible. The books of the Tanakh are the same as, but are not arranged in the same order as Christian Bibles.

tefillah – prayer

Torah – the first five books of the Bible, misunderstood as "law" in English translations. The Torah is more accurately God's teaching and instruction. It contains topics such as science, history, priestly procedures, civil statutes, ordinances, health, agriculture, commandments, prophecies, prayer, animal husbandry, architecture, civics, and many others. The root word of Torah comes from the Hebrew word *yarah*, which means "to hit the mark." Torah may also be used to refer to all of the Hebrew Bible, or even to its smallest meaning, a procedure. Torah may be used by Messianic Jews to refer to the entire Bible from Genesis to Revelation, for the Torah is the foundation for all the Scriptures. The Prophets point Israel back to the Torah. The Psalms teach one to love the Torah as King David loved it. The Writings teach the consequences of departing from the Torah and the rewards for returning to it. The New Testament brings the Torah to its fullest meaning in the person Yeshua the Messiah, and much of the New Testament quotes the Tanakh.

tzakanim – elders

tzitzit – fringes attached to the corners of a garment that are to remind the wearer to keep the commandments

yarmulke – another name for the cap of a Jewish male

Yeshua – Jesus. His name means "salvation."

1

THE MESSIANIC PATTERN OF WORSHIP

The Messianic Movement derives from various backgrounds. It is one of the most racially diverse religious groups in the United States, and it is considered a "grassroots" movement. The Messianic Movement is a growing phenomenon, both within the United States and worldwide. Many traditional Christians are now choosing to keep the Biblical Feasts, so there are even more non-Jewish Messianic fellowships today than Jewish.

Messianic worship has the potential to be a fulfilling and profound experience. Although Messianic congregations and fellowships are springing up all over the world, the diversity of religious, ethnic, and academic backgrounds makes every congregation different, whether primarily Jewish or Gentile. There is no all-inclusive pattern for Messianic worship, so the best approach is to describe the more usual components of a service.

Like the first disciples and apostles of Yeshua (Jesus), no one really knows what to call this movement. Although it is often called the "Messianic Movement," that's a bit of a misnomer. Those who follow Messiah Yeshua are Messianic, but then again, so are observant Jews. Although Orthodox Jews do not believe that Yeshua is the Messiah, they nevertheless await and pray for Messiah's coming daily, so they, too, are Messianic in expectation. The difference is that Orthodox Jews are looking for the Messiah's first coming, but "Messianics" are looking for his return.

In the First Century, believers in the Messiahship of Yeshua were called by many names: The Way, The Nazarenes, and eventually, Christians, a name that is reflected today by saying "Messianic." Since most people understand that a Christian is a follower of Yeshua, people today also understand that a "Messianic" is a follower of Yeshua. This does not make the Orthodox Jew any less messianic in his or her expectation.

Modern Messianics trace their history back to the very beginning of Christianity, but they particularly identify with the early Nazarenes. Epiphanius of Salamis, a 3rd Century Bishop, described Nazarenes as having the following practices:

1. They use both Old and New Testaments
2. They have good knowledge of Hebrew and use the Old Testament; they read at least one gospel in Hebrew.
3. They believe in resurrection of the dead.
4. They believe that God is the Creator of all things.
5. They believe in God and His son Jesus Christ.
6. They observe the Law of Moses.
7. They originated in Jerusalem and later fled to Pella before 70.
8. They were located geographically in Pella, Kokaba, and Coele Syria.

The Nazarenes were not considered heretical by the Church until the 4th Century. Augustine of Hippo (354-430 AD) marks a turning point in the history of the Church's view of Nazarenes. Augustine's acceptance of Epiphanius' judgment fixed their fate and led to their final rejection by the Christian Church. Augustine says about the Nazarenes: "They profess to be Christians and profess that Christ is the Son of God, they practice baptism, they keep the old law, specifically circumcision, Sabbath observance, food restrictions, and are few in number." Jerome states that the Nazarenes existed into the early 5th Century.

Although diverse, modern Messianic Judaism is generally understood to be a movement of Jews and Gentiles committed to the Messiahship of Jesus. Messianic Jews practice the perpetuation of Jewish life and tradition. Identification with the Jewish people and Israel is central to their ethnic and spiritual identities. They are committed both to the Jewish people and the larger Body of Messiah (Christ).

Messianics place a great importance upon Torah observance and the relationship between the Old and New Covenants. They do not see Torah observance as a requirement for salvation; rather, they see it as an outgrowth of salvation called sanctification. Messianics don't promote a works-based salvation, but a covenantal relationship of loving obedience.

Messianic Judaism has been described as the "third rail" between Judaism and Christianity, and non-Jewish Messianics also walk that rail, yet without so much ethnic Jewish tradition. Messianics confess that *Yeshua* (Jesus) is the *Mashiach* (Messiah) both to Messianic Jews and Christians.

2

THE FACILITY

A sanctuary may include congregational seating, a *bimah*, a *mikveh*, and an ark (*aron*). A bimah is similar to a pulpit, but it is designed for the reading of the Scriptures as well as the teaching of the Word. For this reason the bimah is larger than a traditional pulpit so that the Torah scroll can be unrolled for reading. It is sometimes called the "Seat of Moses." A mikveh is a gathering of waters for immersion, and it is known to Christians as a baptistry. Immersion may mark many life events, not just salvation. Since the requirements of a mikveh include "living water," the mikveh may have a slightly different design.

The ark contains scrolls of Torah and other Scriptures, such as the scroll (*megillah*) of Esther. The scrolls represent Yeshua, the Living Word, who is the Word made flesh that dwelled among us. The ark may have a *ner tamid*, which is a perpetual light reminding congregants of the menorah that lit the entryway to the Holy of Holies where the Torah was maintained. The ark may also have a curtain (*parokhet*), and the Torah scroll itself can be decorated with a beautifully embroidered mantle and even a "crown."

A congregation may have a fellowship hall and kitchen to accommodate a common meal called *oneg* following the service.

Why so Jewish?

Synagogue services have changed very little in the past 2000 years, and even today a Shabbat service gives a glimpse into what Yeshua and his disciples experienced. Because the language of the Orthodox Jewish prayer service and many Messianic congregations is Hebrew, an "unprepared visitor has little insight into what is transpiring...everyone seems to be standing, sitting, bowing, reciting, and moving about in a way that seems unfamiliar and random." (Hizak, 1988, p. 5) The objective of this booklet is to guide the visitor through this unfamiliar territory so that he or she can appreciate the ancient, yet beautiful traditions experienced in a Messianic worship service.

Like a synagogue, a Messianic fellowship does not require a specific type of building. The primary function of the building is to facilitate the reading and study of the Torah, the Word of God. It enables believers to assemble on Shabbat and at the appointed feasts (*moedim*) [1] of Israel: "Not forsaking the assembling of ourselves together, as the manner of some is; but exhorting one another: and so much the more, as you see the day approaching." (Hebrews 10:25 KJV)

The pattern of worship usually is derived from Scripture and from the "traditions (customs) of the fathers" passed down through Judaism, the roots of the faith. Traditions can be good or bad, and Scripture is the guide. Paul, the great Jewish rabbi, apostle, and author, wrote that there are good traditions we should uphold:

> Therefore, brethren, stand fast, and hold the traditions which you have been taught, whether by word, or our epistle. (2 Thessalonians 2:2)

1. Exodus 23:17; 34:23; Deuteronomy 16:16

> Now I praise you because you remember me in everything and hold firmly to the traditions, just as I

delivered them to you. (1 Corinthians
11:2)

The Greek word for "traditions" is *paradosis* (Strongs #3862), which specifically refers to procedures and decisions based on the Jewish oral law, not the written Word. Since Paul passed on Jewish congregational traditions to the righteous Gentiles of Thessalonica and Corinth, there is richness within synagogue practice from which Messianics draw. Within the same context that he validates the letters of the apostles as guidelines for believers, Paul places emphasis on keeping the Jewish traditions.

Yeshua had the Jewish custom of going to the synagogue every Sabbath to worship even though this custom was not expressly given as a commandment: "He went to Nazareth, where he had been brought up, and on the Sabbath day he went into the synagogue as was his custom. And he stood up to read." (Luke 4:16) All of the apostles, including Paul, followed Yeshua's example; his customs were their customs. Yeshua's last instructions on earth to his disciples were to teach his Father's commandments and ways to all nations [2].

Scripture can speak very strongly against bad traditions. Yeshua addresses these in Matthew 15:6 by saying "...you have made the commandment of God of no effect by your tradition." And in Mark 7:8 "You have let go of the commands of God and are holding on to the traditions of men." Yeshua teaches that it is not good to hold onto a tradition, yet to let go of the actual written Word.

The simple test of whether a tradition is good or bad is whether it leads a disciple into rendering the written commandment of God powerless or powerful. Yeshua gave his disciples some tests for customs and traditions with which to determine a custom's validity.

While there is definitely a problem with substituting tradition for the actual written Word, there is no conflict between truth and tradition when the tradition grows from the seed of the Word. Such a tradition produces

2. Matthew
28:20;
1 Corinthians
11:1; Acts 17:2;
Acts 26:3)

17

harmony that exalts the actual Scripture. The tradition, like the fruit, becomes the vehicle for the observance of the truth, giving it expression and life in a dynamic world. A BEKY Book is available for a more thorough look at the relationship between truth and tradition.

The desire of a congregation is not just to talk about Yeshua's walk, but to walk as He walked. "...this is how we know we are in Him: whoever claims to live in him must walk as Yeshua did." (1 John 2:5-6) This includes patterning our worship after the way Yeshua worshiped and the patterns of the Eternal Word.

In his book, *God's Appointed Times*, Messianic Rabbi Barney Kasdan states:

> The typical service, while having flexibility, has followed the same basic structure since the days of Ezra and Nehemiah (Neh. 8). There are opening praise psalms and hymns largely based on the Book of Psalms, along with rabbinic reading, followed by the public reading/chanting from the scrolls of the Torah (Law) and the Haftorah (Prophets)...A third major section of the service is a sermon on the passage for that week. After a closing hymn, the service ends with the Oneg Shabbat (delight of the Sabbath)."

Mezuzah

In most Messianic facilities, there is a small, rectangular box or cylinder on the doorframe of the entry door or other doorways. A Hebrew letter *shin* (c) usually identifies the decorative container; the shin stands for *El Shaddai*, one of the names of God. There is also an acrostic in the name El Shaddai that in Hebrew translates to: "Keeper of the doors of Israel."

Inside the mezuzah are parchments with key verses related to the commandments to place the Word on the doorposts of one's house and gates in Deuteronomy 6:9 and 11:20. The texts of Deuteronomy 6:4-9 and 11:13-21 are written by a *sofer* (scribe) on tiny parchments and inserted into the box.

The mezuzah is a sign that a Jewish family lives inside that home, and in a synagogue or Messianic congregation, the mezuzah means the same. It is a reminder that as Psalm 121:8 states, El Shaddai will watch our coming and going. Because it holds the Holy Scriptures, you may see some congregants touch their fingers to the mezuzah as a sign of reverence for the Word.

3

ORDER OF SERVICE

There is no standard order of service among Messianic congregations, but there are several standard components that may comprise the experience. "Shabbat Shalom" is the standard greeting on the Sabbath. Its meaning goes well beyond just a greeting. When we say it, we are imparting a blessing: "May you have complete wellness, wholeness, rest, completion, and peace in God's creation!" This sets the tone for joy.

Shofar

Sounding the *Shofar* (Ram's Horn) is part of many Messianic Shabbat services. Some shofars are made from the smaller goat horns, and they typically produce a higher-pitched sound. Some are longer horns taken from kudu or other deer, and they are longer and may have graceful twists, producing a deeper sound. The shofar served many purposes in ancient Israel. It was sounded to warn of attacks, to announce the arrival of the king, to call the army to march, to alert the faithful to repentance, to announce the arrival of the Sabbath and new months, and much more. Although Orthodox Jewish synagogues do not sound the shofar on the weekly Shabbat, reserving it for set times, Messianic congregations tend to blow the shofar much more freely!

The sounding of the shofar to call God's people to assemble is established in Leviticus 23 and affirmed in Hebrews 10:25. The shofar has a great Messianic meaning for us today. Its sound will be heard announcing Messiah's second coming that awakens the dead, calling them and those who are alive to meet Yeshua in the air [3].

Liturgical Prayer

Every Shabbat we say a few of the ancient prayers that Yeshua, the apostles, and early believers said, and more often sang, when they worshiped in the synagogue. These liturgical prayers are either quotations entirely of Scripture or based on similarly-themed Scriptural passages. In their Passover *seder*, Yeshua and the disciples sang the traditional liturgical Psalms for the service. Yeshua taught his disciples a liturgical prayer commonly called "The Lord's Prayer" that is characterized by the collective pronouns "our," "us," and "we." Corporate prayer emphasizes "we," while personal prayers reflect individual needs, and both are important in one's prayer life.

In Acts 3:1, the apostles continued to gather in the Temple to say the prayers. Liturgical prayer is the believer's way of affirming that he identifies with the Body of Messiah; he does not stand aloof [4]. Liturgical prayers from ancient times, such as the Song of Moses, will be sung in eternity, [5] and the Psalms identify the set prayers that were sung at specified times in the Temple service.

The same ancient prayers are still being said today in synagogues around the world with great sentiment and solidarity. Some of these prayers are the Shema (Hear, O Israel/The Greatest Commandment), and the Amidah/Shmonei Esrei (Standing Prayer). These prayers are important because Yeshua and the disciples modeled them, and they remind us to bless, acknowledge, and thank our Father for what He has done for each of us through Yeshua. In these prayers,

3. I Thessalonians 4:16

4. Galatians 2:12; 1 Corinthians 12

5. Revelation 15:3

there is no room to draw attention to ourselves, but only to bless and exalt God.

The Shema is based on Deut. 6:4-6, the greatest commandment. We acknowledge God's sovereignty, His kingship, and gladly accept His commandments and covenant as well as responsibility to love our neighbor: "Hear O Israel, the LORD your God, the LORD is One, and you shall love the LORD your God with all your heart, soul, and strength..." When Yeshua was asked what was the greatest commandment, he cited the Shema and the commandment from Leviticus to love one's neighbor; therefore, in many Messianic congregations, the phrase "And you shall love your neighbor as yourself" is added at the end of the Shema.

The Amidah (ah-me-dah') for Sabbath is a congregational prayer in the siddur (see-dur'; prayerbook) with parts dating back to Ezra's day. The Amidah is the framework of prayer for the three-times-daily [6] prayer of the regular week. A modified form of the Amidah is prayed on Shabbat and festival days, and typically the congregation turns toward Jerusalem. If you would like to know why we turn toward Jerusalem, turn to Frequently Asked Questions in the back of this booklet.

Jewish tradition encourages the worshiper to take three steps backward, then three steps forward, which is symbolically acknowledging that one is stepping into the Presence of Adonai. The prayer leader will prompt you. *Standing With Israel: A House of Prayer for All Nations* is a book that explains the Hebrew daily prayers and their prophetic implications in more detail.

In many Messianic Shabbat prayerbooks, the Hebrew text is given along with the English text, and possibly a transliteration, so that it is possible to pray with understanding. A siddur may be considered a combination prayerbook and songbook, for most of the prayers may be sung.

6. 9:00 a.m., 3:00 p.m., and after sundown.

23

The siddur is saturated with passages from Scripture. As an example, one Torah portion, [7] Va'etchanan (Deuteronomy 3:23-7:11), supplies the following to the daily and Shabbat prayers in the siddur:

- 4:4 is recited immediately before the reading of the Torah
- 4:39 is found in the *Aleinu* prayer for Shabbat
- 4:44 is recited by the congregation when the Torah scroll is held up after the reading.
- Chapter Five lists the Ten Commandments, also included in the daily siddur
- 6:4-9 is the *Shema* and *V'ahavta*, which are prayed twice daily
- 6:4-9 contain the Scriptural rationale for the use of items such as the *mezuzah* (commandments   on the doorpost) and *tefillin* (phylacteries)
- 6:21 is found in the traditional Passover order of service.

Questions about Hebrew prayer are common from non-Jews who begin to see Yeshua in the Torah; they know that they are not to become Jewish, so how much Jewish tradition is necessary? It's perfectly understandable to be cautious about trading one set of traditions for another without evaluating the purpose, source, and Scriptural foundation.

7. A "Torah portion" is also called the weekly sidra or parashah. In synagogues, the Torah is read annually in chronological portions, so Jews all over the world read the same section of Torah and the Prophets each week until the entire Torah is read.

Start with the understanding that whether you do or don't participate in corporate Hebrew prayer, it does not affect salvation or right standing with Yeshua. It will more likely affect one's relationship with his brothers and sisters in Messiah Yeshua. To stand with someone is to pray with him or her.

It is important to address whether corporate prayer has value to the modern believers. Corporate, or liturgical, prayers are prayers said or sung collectively, such as the liturgical songs and prayers in the Psalms. This practice is common to almost all churches, and it shouldn't invoke fear. After all, if one attends a typical church, and the worship leader announces that the first song is "Amazing Grace," then everyone sings "Amazing Graze." Each individual doesn't turn to his or her favorite song in the hymnbook and start singing it!

Corporate prayer enhances brotherhood and fosters a more shared, united experience. It is perhaps when those prayers involve collective body movement other than close-your-eyes-and-bow-your-head that non-Jews can experience trepidation.

It is a given that human beings fear what they do not understand. While learning about the background and Biblical significance of Hebrew prayer can remove the fear of "vain repetition," the fear of a new language can remain.

Because the Jews have guarded and protected the Torah and Shabbat with their very lives for thousands of years, the privileges and obligations of worship devolved upon them, as Paul acknowledges in Romans 9:

> ...my kinsmen according to the flesh,
> who are Israelites, to whom belongs the
> adoption as sons, and the glory and
> the covenants and the giving of the
> Law and the temple service and the
> promises, whose are the fathers, and
> from whom is the Christ according to
> the flesh, who is over all, God blessed
> forever. Amen. (Romans 9:3-5)

Goble explains, "Modern scholars such as Bousset, Oesterley, Baumstart and Werner have shown that the early Messianic community functioned liturgically very much like a synagogue." (p. 28) The earliest church was completely Jewish, for this was the plan of Heaven.

If one people-group was given this scepter since the reception of the Covenant, then some of the ethos of worshipping the God of Abraham, Isaac, and Jacob will be Jewish. If one attends a Messianic Jewish synagogue, he or she should expect this style of worship; Yeshua didn't change the Temple prayers or times of worship, neither should newcomers expect to "fix" a style of worship they don't yet understand. In a non-Jewish Messianic congregation, one may find more of a blend of church and synagogue customs.

Evangelical Christian worship is likely to be just as remote an experience to a Jew who has always worshipped in a synagogue. What the Christian considers a move of the Holy Spirit, the Jew may identify as a whirlwind of soul music that depends upon feelings to function. To the Jew, the hushed prayers of the Amidah are attuned to hear the Spirit in a "still, small voice. [8]" Both reflect culture, and each strives to establish that relationship with Heaven.

Absorbing the beauty of the worship customs experienced by Yeshua can be wonderfully personal and pleasant. Liturgical prayer is not as rigid as it may appear. Although Orthodox Christians are accustomed to liturgical prayer, evangelicals may see liturgical prayer as vain repetition.

> But when ye pray, use not vain repetitions, as the heathen [do]: for they think that they shall be heard for their much speaking. (Matthew 6:7 KJV)

In an interlinear Greek text, there is no corresponding word in the text as is translated "vain." It is the word for "repetition" that is in the Greek text, and it means to repeat over and over. Had Yeshua said, "Don't pray the same thing over and over," and that was all he said concerning repetition, then he would be stating something in opposition to the Scriptural pattern in the Psalms, where a phrase is often repeated for emphasis, such as "His mercy endures forever."

Yeshua, however, explains completely what he means within the context of the verse. He says that a "[vain]

8. I Kings 19:1-12

26

repetition" is to think God will hear you simply because you pile a lot of words into the prayer. Maybe The Repeater even thinks that men will hear much speaking and think him pious, which serves his own ego, not God. English teachers call this "padding," and it occurs when a student has little to say, but he adds lots of words to make an essay appear longer than the actual content. The cure for this is to warn that the student will have to pay $1 for every unnecessary word. It may be unenforceable, but it sends the message, especially when the teacher totals the "bill" alongside the grade or subtracts the bill from the grade!

Although Yeshua singles out heathens as the culprits in superstitious prayer, in ancient times, there were also some apostate Jews who believed in dual powers. These apostates "always doubled certain words in their prayers; and they [the rabbis] issued warnings to those who read the text by proceeding from the last word to the first, probably for reasons of a magical character." (Golli, 1950, p. 135)

Taken in context, Yeshua is cautioning against using repetitious prayers as magical formulas or for false piety. Compare Matthew 6:7 to the parable in Luke 18:1-18, which describes the balanced role that repetition plays in prayer. Prayer should be relational, not a speech well-crafted and presented for accolades, and even the daily prayer is to be prayed with *kavanah*, or passion.

One misconception of Jewish prayer is based on limited observation or education about Jewish worship. In a class this author attended, a rabbi told the class that a person who repeats a prayer is praying vain repetition. This is consistent with the fear of many non-Jews who visit a Messianic congregation and see people praying from a prayerbook. So what did the rabbi mean? The rabbi went on to explain the Jewish viewpoint of praying set prayers. Even though the same prayers are offered three times daily, the person is changed by the prayers, so they are not the same! To simply repeat the words every day is unacceptable!

Prayer involves judging one's self according to the standard of the Word contained in those prayers, and the person who prays sincerely is changed by the Word. Scripture is re-read over a person's lifetime, and it never becomes boring, for each time the Scripture is read through again, the person has aged both chronologically as well as spiritually. He uncovers new truths each time he reads the same passage anew. Prayer is like this. Believers are transformed by the Spirit, so when one repeats earlier petitions and praises, the prayers are not new, but they are completely renewed in us!

From the Jewish point of view as explained by Rabbi Tatz, prayer (*tefillah*) [9] is the process of changing one's self. While some of the prayers may seem to be a daily shopping list of goodies that one requests from the Father, it is through the process of prayer that the self-judgment of "*hitpallel*" [10] occurs. It is perfectly possible that one may pray the prayers as merely a list of wants, but the point of prayer is to judge one's self in relation to those requests. If the Father granted this, would I use it for me or for Him? Would I enrich myself or enrich the Body of Messiah?

Since this is an internal process, only the Holy Spirit can discern whether the transformation of the soul is occurring in prayer. Rabbi Tatz stated in a class lecture, "If you mumble a few words, it has no effect at all...You work on yourself to become somebody that you weren't before. You sacrifice the person you were before." Since we now bring the "calves of our lips" instead of Temple sacrifices, the words reflect the person we want to become, dissolving the disobedience into ashes on the altar. Because the soul has

9. Pronounce very quickly, running together the t and f sounds: tfee-lah.

10. Heet-pah-lel: "To judge one's self." Prayer in Hebrew is to examine one's self; the publican that Yeshua compared to the Pharisee was the one who was praying according to the definition of prayer; the Pharisee was not judging himself, but comparing himself to another.

> **Prayers cannot change the** past. **By changing the** *person*, **the prayers change the** future.

subordinated itself to the Father's will, then the result is satisfying to His will. One destroys on the altar of prayer anything which impairs unity with the Father's will.

A thorough examination of ancient or modern Jewish texts on prayer yields a consistent approach to prayer as one of *kavanah* [11]. While to an outsider the prayers may have a rote or dispassionate appearance, no Jew has been instructed to pray dispassionately. It is possible that any individual, Jew or Gentile, may pray rote prayers, yet judging the sincerity or passion of the prayer from the exterior appearance is a mistake.

> Our Sages taught us that there are two levels of prayer: regular prayers, which appear in the siddur and are said at set times by Jews all over the world, and pleas, which are prayers from the heart that each individual composes him/herself, when s/he feels the need. This siddur contains traditional and new prayers. Some were composed hundreds of years ago, and some in recent times. The siddur also includes songs, readings and questions to inspire individual prayer. The siddur is intended to help one who prays to incorporate both kinds of prayers. (The World of Prayer, Preparing for Prayer, Vol. 1, for **Grades 3-6**. Jerusalem: KLN)

From a Jewish child's earliest education in prayer, the intention is never for him or her to neglect prayers from the heart in favor of corporate prayers. Both are introduced and encouraged. How many non-Jewish families teach eight-year-old children the importance and process of prayer in such depth? An invitation to appreciate or engage in Hebrew prayer is not an invitation to an empty tradition; it connects the believer to the past and can be a map to future growth.

11. directed, intentional passion and sincerity

29

Prayer and Psalms in Hebrew

Hebrew prayer is in a foreign language, so it seems strange to the English-speaker at first. Yes, it is a foreign language, but in Hebrew, the word (*dvar*) is the thing (*dvar*) and the language of Creation. It is the language of Adonai's most important message to mankind. In other languages, the word is merely a label corresponding to the thing. In Hebrew, it IS the thing! This may sound mysterious, but Hebrew words are made of pictograms that tell the story of the word's actual essence and significance to man. It is the English-speaker who speaks a foreign language to the original pages of Scripture, and this explains why so many English translations are made to "speak in a known tongue."

While one does not have to learn Hebrew to be saved or study Scripture, the ability to study in Hebrew certainly enhances the experience. The Psalms, which are designed for corporate worship and extend to all life events, have a unique feature that emphasizes their structure and aids memorization for recitation in the synagogue, Temple, congregation, or personal prayer. Psalm 119 is broken into numbered thematic categories according to Hebrew letters.

Psalm 145, the *Ashrei*, is a song easily memorized if one uses the acrostic of the Hebrew letters. In order to use those acrostic memory aids, however, the prayer has to be sung in Hebrew, not English. The Ashrei includes the statement, "Every day I will bless you." Does He get tired of being blessed? Another line from the Psalm is "A recollection of Your abundant goodness they will utter..." Again?

The Psalmists acknowledge repetition in prayer is important. Whether we find it boring or not is not the point. Whether it is His will and His pattern in prayer matters, and the Hebrew letters help to fix the concepts in one's soul, for to pray is to pray from the Spirit (*Ruach*). The Spirit is not dependent upon a feeling to pray the words of Scripture on a given day; the Spirit understands "It is written," and praying Psalms is written. It is the soul (*nefesh*) that is being dealt with in prayer, for the Spirit naturally reaches to connect with its source, the Holy Spirit (Ruach HaKodesh).

Etiquette

Great care is given to siddurim [12] because they are full of Scripture. In fact, old Torah scrolls are not thrown away, but buried! Siddurim also are given great consideration and treated with extreme tenderness. A Jew will never place a siddur or a *Tanakh* (Bible) on the floor or put some other object on top of them. The Word of God is given great respect in its written form. This is an excellent object lesson on how the Body of Messiah is to treat one another, in whom the Word of God is carried. We are instructed to greet one another with a "holy kiss." [13]

Likewise, a Jew may kiss the cover of his siddur upon taking out his or her siddur or upon the conclusion of prayers. Should the siddur accidentally be dropped on the floor, the owner will pick it up quickly, dust it off, and kiss it as a sign of respect. To the Western mind, this may look odd, but in the Near and Middle East, kissing something is still a sign of respect or value. When two acquaintances meet, they will kiss each side of the other's face in greeting.

Again, while this is not customary in Western countries, the Bible and the Hebrew prayers were birthed in the context of ancient Israel and Judaism; therefore, the customs associated are from that culture. The custom should not be viewed ethnocentrically, but placed in a cultural context in which a kiss denotes value, not idolatry.

On a practical level, if non-Jews participate with their Jewish brothers and sisters in prayer, it would be a kindness if they did not place Bibles or prayer books on the floor or place other objects or books on top of them. Doing so sends an unintentional message of disrespect

12. plural of siddur

13. Romans 16:16; 1 Corinthians 16:20; 2 Corinthians 13:12; 1 Thessalonians 5:26

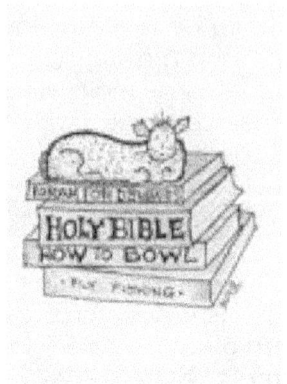

for God's Word. It's also a good habit to acquire, for it can function as an object lesson to teach children the authority of God's Word and its importance in our lives.

Standing during prayer is a sign of respect; the only seat in the Temple was Adonai's judgment seat. To sit when others stand to pray sends a silent message of negative judgment or disrespect for those praying. It is equally disrespectful to leave the room or retreat to the door.

Blessings

If it seems as though everything involves a blessing in a Messianic Shabbat service, it does! In the Creation week, Adonai set apart the Sabbath in three foundational ways (Gen. 2:2-3):

> a) He rested
> b) He blessed it
> c) He sanctified it (made it holy)

Shabbat services also should be characterized by these three things.

Rest is the cessation of creative work, and for further study, it is suggested that one do a Strong's search on the different words for "work" in Scripture to see them in their contexts and compare them. In the local congregation, "rest" is possible when we "bake what you will bake and boil what you will boil" (Exodus 16:23) before Shabbat. If necessary, we hold those foods warm or reheat the cooked food. Crockpots or stovetop warmers are ideal for holding cooked foods warm on Shabbat.

Blessing the Shabbat is the second foundational

component, and worshipers say blessings over each part of the service to mirror the Father's Shabbat activity. There are blessings in the prayers, blessings in the songs, blessings over the Scripture readings, blessings over bread and fruit of the vine, blessings over children, well... blessings over everything! Isn't it wonderful to have a sanctuary day where you hear the opposite of the cursing that assaults the ears in the workplace, streets, and other places we visit during the workweek?

By resting and blessing the Shabbat, believers mirror Elohim's final action: we make holy the day in our own lives by choice, with effort, and in love. While He has already made the day holy, the question is, "Will I?" Will the Creation follow His Word, "Be holy, for I am holy?" Holiness is not just being set apart, it is being set apart in order to gather to like kind and like mind so that all Creation mirrors the holiness in Heaven above. This is how Yeshua taught his disciples to pray, "May Your will be done on Earth as it is in Heaven." Holiness is imitation of the Divine will, and this should characterize every Shabbat.

Davidic Praise - Song and Dance

Messianic-style worship songs are usually based on the Psalms or other Scripture. Some congregations may incorporate contemporary Christian praise and worship. Musical instruments and singing have always been an integral part of worshiping the Holy One of Israel:

> These are the men David put in charge of the music in the House of the LORD after the ark came to rest there. They ministered with music before the tabernacle, the Tent of Meeting, until Solomon built the temple of the LORD in Jerusalem. (1 Chronicles 6:31-32)
>
> David told the leaders of the Levites to appoint their brothers as singers to sing joyful songs, accompanied by musical

instruments: lyres, harps, and cymbals.
(1 Chronicles 15:16)

Along with singing and music, some fellowships have Hebraic dance. Dancing can be seen throughout Scripture. Dancing should be done decently, in modest decorum, and with a heart and attitude of worship. Ecclesiastes 3:4 states that there is: "A time to weep and a time to laugh, a time to mourn, and a time to dance." The prophet Jeremiah speaks of a time when "...maidens will dance and be glad, young men and old as well. I will turn their mourning into gladness; I will give them comfort and joy instead of sorrow." (Jer. 31:13)

Sharing Revelation

> "What is it then, brothers? When you come together, each one of you has a psalm, has a teaching, has a revelation, has another language, has an interpretation. Let all things be done to build each other up. If any man speaks in another language, let it be two, or at the most three, and in turn; and let one interpret. But if there is no interpreter, let him keep silence in the assembly, and let him speak to himself, and to God. Let the prophets speak, two or three, and let the others discern. But if a revelation is made to another sitting by, let the first keep silence. For you all can prophesy one by one, that all may learn, and all may be exhorted. The spirits of the prophets are subject to the prophets, for God is not a God of confusion, but of shalom." (I Cor. 14:26-33)

Some congregations may offer an opportunity for individuals, as gifted and led by the Holy Spirit, to edify the Body of Messiah. We believe that Paul is not prohibiting women from using their spiritual gifts in public in I Corinthians 14:35, but addressing a specific problem within the Corinthian congregation where some women were causing disruptions by asking questions at inappropriate times. Something caused them not to "hold their peace," which would have been disruptive no matter whether a man or a woman interrupted the service.

History provides some perspective, and it explains why some women did not have experience in a synagogue or believers' gathering. Even into the 1900s, women in the Middle East often were not taught to read. Typically they married at between twelve and fourteen years of age, and they stayed at home with their children while their husbands went to synagogue for prayer, Scripture reading, and a lesson on the weekly Torah portion. The husbands would return and reteach the rabbi's lesson to his wife and children. It is not surprising that women, who previously may not have had experience in the synagogue setting, would have made a faux pas as they tried to participate and find out what was going on!

If Paul were prohibiting all women from speaking at a public meeting, then he would have contradicted himself in I Corinthians 11:5 where he states: "And every woman who prays or prophesies..." One cannot remain silent and prophesy at the same time! Other Scripture states that women will speak and glorify God: "...it shall come to pass in the last days, says God, I will pour out of my Spirit upon all flesh: and your sons and daughters shall prophesy" (Acts 2:17; Joel 2:28). "The Lord gives the commandment; the women who proclaim the gospel are a great host..." (Psalm 68:11) Another case of women prophesying is in Acts 21:8-9: "Philip the evangelist...and the same man had four daughters, virgins, which did prophesy." The female voice is vital within the Body of Messiah, and it is cherished by the Father.

Blessing of the Children

Children are invited to gather under the *tallit* (prayer shawl) for a blessing. The blessing for boys is "May Adonai make you as Ephraim and Manasseh," and for girls, "May Adonai make you as Sarah, Rebecca, Rachel, and Leah."

Torah Processional

As precious as a Torah scroll is to a congregation, it cannot compare to the joy we have in our Messiah, Yeshua, who IS the Word made flesh that dwells among us. For this reason, the congregation may march in a processional behind this representation of God's Word accompanied by music, shofars, dance, banners, flags, tambourines, and any other instrument of praise and worship. Carry your own Bible if you have one! If you have not experienced processional worship before, you may find the pattern in the Psalms of Ascent, David's processional with the ark of the covenant, and Yeshua's triumphant entry into Jerusalem. Enjoy it!

In many congregations, one person will carry the Torah scroll throughout the congregation. You may notice congregants touching the fringes of their *tallits* to the scroll and kissing the fringes (*tzitzit*) in affection, and others may touch a *siddur* (prayerbook) to the scroll and kiss the siddur to express affection for the Word of God.

It is acceptable and respectful to remain standing and to sing or clap along as the Word of God goes before us. At the conclusion of the processional, the scroll is unrolled if a reader will be reading the Hebrew text that Shabbat. If not, the scroll will remain covered and the Torah portion will be read in English.

Some people will touch the Torah scroll and then kiss their fingers during the Torah processional, and they may back away from the scroll. Kissing as an affectionate greeting is admittedly more of an ancient Near/Middle Eastern custom that has been transplanted in the American synagogue service as a sign of affection for God's Word. However, in Modern Israel, it is still customary to greet a friend or family member by exchanging a brief kiss on both cheeks. Touching the Torah scroll and bringing it to your lips is also a symbolic act of affection for the Word of God. At least four times in Psalms 119, King David exclaims, "How I love Your Torah!"

We may sometimes laugh if we see someone who has lost an important object kiss it happily when it is found, but to the person who has found that precious object, who cares if someone laughs? We, too, are recovering the Torah in our generation, a precious thing that was lost.

Some people do not turn their backs on the scroll as another symbolic act. If we symbolically follow the Word of God in our processional as a sign of our intent to follow it with our whole heart, then symbolically we do not turn our backs on His Word. The intention of our hearts is to always respect that Word. In fact, one of the seven spirits of God listed in Isaiah is *Yirat Adonai*, or The Reverence of Adonai.

In Israel today, you'll see something similar at the Kotel (Wailing Wall). When Jews conclude their prayers, they do not simply turn their backs and walk away. They back up to a certain point before turning away from the former site of the Temple as a sign of reverence for the Presence of Adonai. As a reminder, there may be a banner in the front of the sanctuary that reads, "Know Before Whom You Stand." The familiar endearment of a kiss is balanced with proper reverence for the Presence of God.

While you will see many symbolic acts as well as Jewish or Christian symbols in a Messianic congregation, the great Rabbi Abraham Heschel said, "Symbols are superfluous: the Sabbath is itself the symbol." Symbols merely remind a believer of the holiness of the day.

Reading the Torah, Haftorah, and Brit HaChadasha

Each Shabbat is a public reading from the Scriptures: the *Torah* (Books of Moses/Law,) the *Haftorah* (Books of the Prophets) and the *Brit HaChadasha* (Renewed Covenant). Messianics read selected passages from the Torah and the Prophets every Sabbath as was done in Yeshua's day. This selected reading is called the *parashah*. Additionally, Messianics also read from the New Testament (Renewed Covenant).

Reading the Scriptures on a set schedule is an ancient practice. Yeshua attended synagogue and read the selected Scripture aloud in Luke 4:16-17, "...as his custom was, he went into the synagogue on the Sabbath day, and **stood up for to read**. The scroll of the prophet Isaiah was handed to him." It was not by chance that this scroll was the Book of Isaiah. A portion of Isaiah was the scheduled reading for that Shabbat.

The public reading of Scripture dates back to Moses when he commanded the people to read them aloud at a religious gathering (Deut. 31:11-12). In Nehemiah 8, Ezra reemphasized the public reading as well as "...making it clear and giving the meaning so that the people could understand what was being read." Both Messianic Jews and Gentiles were expected to attend synagogue to "hear Moses," for Acts 15:21 documents the expectation that all would follow that tradition in order to hear the Scriptures; only the wealthiest of families could afford a scroll of the Torah, Prophets, or Writings (including Psalms). If you are physically able, remain standing during the reading of the Torah since that was the pattern of respect set in the Book of Nehemiah.

In Acts 13:14-16, Paul, as was his custom with his companions, goes "...into the synagogue on the Sabbath day, and sat down. And after the reading of the law and prophets..." Paul participates in the traditional Shabbat service, and he admonishes

Timothy: "Until I come, devote yourself to the public reading of the Scripture, to preaching, and to teaching." (I Timothy 4:13). The Scripture referred to here is the Older Covenant (*Tanakh*). The Renewed Covenant (New Testament) as it is now was not recognized by the Church until 367 A.D.

Are there more reasons why believers should read the Torah and Prophets on Shabbat? In Acts 15, the apostles meet to discuss those born Gentiles leaving paganism to follow Yeshua:

> It is my judgment, therefore, that we should not make it difficult for the Gentiles who are turning to God. Instead we should write to them, telling them to abstain from food polluted by idols, from sexual immorality, from the meat of strangled animals, and from blood. For Moses has been preached in every city from the earliest times and is read in the synagogues on every Sabbath.

The implication is that non-Jews will learn the rest and be taught how to be holy and pleasing to God as they attend synagogue every week and hear God's Word read aloud. Pursuing God's Word in the Torah is a blessing, not a yoke, and putting one foot forward at a time is healthy and right.

Torah Message

An elder, pastor, or other leader will teach a message from the Scripture readings. Alternatively, some congregations prefer a "midrash" where one person facilitates the study, and others are free to participate in the discussion over the text.

Praying for the Sick

James 5:14-15 "Is any one of you sick? He should call

the elders of the church to pray over him and anoint him with oil in the name of the Lord. And the prayer offered in faith will make the sick person well; the Lord will raise him up. If he has sinned, he will be forgiven." If you need prayer, please ask the elders to pray for you.

Aaronic Benediction

An elder may bless the congregation according to the pattern of Scripture. Please rise during the blessing and close or avert the eyes from looking directly at the one pronouncing the blessing, for it is Adonai who actually blesses.

Blessing Over the Kiddush

This cup of wine is called the "cup of sanctification." We offer thanksgiving to Him who sanctifies the Shabbat and created all things. We thank Him for the joy He gives us as symbolized by the "wine that gladdens the heart of man" (Psalm 104:15). The blessing is "Blessed are You, O Adonai our God, King of the Universe, who creates the fruit of the vine." Yeshua is The Vine.

Blessing Over the Bread

This blessing is a Sabbath tradition that reminds us of Israel's wilderness experience when on the sixth day God provided a double portion so they could cease from their labor and honor Him on the seventh day. It is a celebration of God's love as shown by His provision in our lives. The blessing is "Blessed are You, O Adonai our God, King of the Universe, Who brings forth The Bread from the earth." The Bread that was raised from the earth was the Bread that was sent from Heaven and resurrected from the dead, our King Messiah Yeshua.

Closing Song

Some congregations may close with a traditional closing song, such as the Sabbath Prayer from "Fiddler on the Roof."

Oneg (Delight) in Shabbat

After the service is breaking of bread in many fellowships. In Judaism, this time was instituted to fulfill Isaiah 58:13-14, "...if you call the Sabbath a delight and the LORD's holy day honorable...then you will find your joy in the LORD." We hope you will take the time not just to eat, but to discuss the Scriptures and ask questions.

Blessing After Meals

The first blessing is unique to the Shabbat meal, and is a Psalm/Song of Ascents. The second blessing is just the first of several that can be made following the meal. The blessing is made after the meal because of the pattern in Deuteronomy 8:10: "When you have eaten and are satisfied, you shall bless the LORD your God for the good land which He has given you."

Offering

In some congregations a traditional offering is taken. In some congregations, a container may be available, and at a certain time in the service, congregants may bring their offerings to drop in the container. In still other congregations, a *tzedekah* (charity) box is located somewhere in the sanctuary. Feel free to drop in an offering or tithe, for Galatians 6:6 reminds us, "And let the one who is taught the word share all good things with him who teaches." We encourage you to share all good things with the Body where you receive nourishment in the Word.

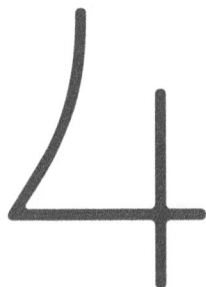

4

HEAD COVERS

Women in some congregations wear a headcovering, whether a scarf, snood, or hat. Women who lead public prayer or operate in the gifts of the Spirit publicly should consider wearing a headcovering to demonstrate proper order in the family, and therefore in Messiah Yeshua. 1 Corinthians 11 gives instructions to Messianic communities about spiritual authority, but Paul also mentions the wearing of headcovers when one ministers within a congregation. In Judaism, only married women cover their heads, but within Gentile congregations, even single women may cover their heads as a sign of reverence for public prayer or the reading of the Holy Scriptures. Customs vary from congregation to congregation and even within congregations.

In some congregations, men wear a cap called a *kippah* (or yarmulke) as a token of respect to the Presence of Adonai in His sanctuary. While Paul seems to be saying in 1 Corinthians 11 that a man was not to cover his head in order to minister within the congregation, a more careful reading of the text in Greek renders Paul's advice as more of a prohibition against cross-dressing. The man was not to wear something hanging down over his head like a female headcover. It was customary for men to wear a headcover in Paul's day, and the priests in the Temple were required to wear them. Indeed, it was a male leper who endured having his head uncovered, so there is no conflict with Paul's instruction and a Jewish male wearing a kippah in the congregation.

5

ORGANIZATIONAL STRUCTURE

A rabbi or pastor and elders may function as the congregational leaders. A *nasi* is the president or overseer of the congregation. Elders (*tzakanim*) may teach, function as the *beit din*, or local congregational court, make *halakah* (set local patterns of custom, praise and worship, community life), lead Shabbat services, and mentor future leaders in the faith of Messiah Yeshua. Another position within a Messianic congregation may be that of deacon (*shammash*). They represent the congregation and assist the elders administratively. Deacons typically oversee the physical premises, ensure the needy are assisted, and actively participate in festival preparation and services.

In congregations that are more ethnically Jewish, there may also be a cantor (*chazzan*) who leads liturgical services, and a *gabbai*, who arranges and supervises the services, appointing a lay prayer leader if necessary.

6

SPECIAL SHABBATS – BAR MITZVAH

If there are young people within a Messianic congregation, then you may find yourself at a bar mitzvah celebration on Shabbat, which is a rite of passage. The congregational celebration of a bar mitzvah is a tradition that marks the addition to the congregation of a son or daughter of Israel who can function and lead competently in the Body of Messiah. After his bar mitzvah, an individual may be called upon to conduct portions of a congregational service. The bar mitzvah may conduct some of the service on the Shabbat of his birthday to demonstrate his readiness for this responsibility.

Bar mitzvah, or "Son of the Commandment," (or Bat Mitzvah, Daughter of the Commandment) is a man-made custom that leads us into keeping and bearing responsibility for God's Word, and is one of many spiritual re-birthdays we may have in our walk with Yeshua as He leads his disicples to the Father. In fact, Yeshua participated in an early form of bar mitzvah when he sat in the Temple courts with the scribes and Torah teachers at the age of twelve.

A bar mitzvah is a rite of passage that marks a developmental milestone. Jewish children in the 1st Century began memorizing the Scriptures when they were five years old, and by the age of twelve, were expected to know both the written Scriptures and the Jewish oral law [14] well enough to converse intelligently with rabbis and scholars.

In the synagogue, each week's Scripture readings are done according to an ancient schedule that includes readings from the Torah (Genesis, Exodus, Leviticus, Numbers, and Deuteronomy), the Prophets, and a Psalm. Additionally, a reading from the Brit HaChadasha (New Testament) is read. Each week's portion has a name; therefore, each person has a "portion in the Torah" that coincides with his or her birthday week. Over the years, a bar mitzvah will become an expert in his birth portion, and he will be able to discuss those Scriptures in depth. He will have read scholarly commentaries, meditated on and prayed about them, taught them, and found new connections to Yeshua our Messiah.

Since Yeshua's custom was to participate in the services of the local synagogue every Sabbath, it is assumed that congregational attendance will be consistent leading up to, and especially AFTER the bar mitzvah. Bar mitzvah is a commitment to the Body of Messiah as much as a commitment to Adonai. Some traditions associated with the bar mitzvah are:

- Family members bring baskets of candy for congregants to throw at the bar/bat mitzvah as he/she approaches the bimah, and all cheer the reading of the Word. The candy is thrown again when the Torah blessing is concluded and after the Haftorah (Prophets) reading. This emphasizes the sweetness of the Word of God, which is sweeter than honey and the honeycomb. Appropriate cheers might be "*Baruch Haba!*" for a male, or "*Baruch Haba-ah!*" for a female, "The Sweetness of the Torah!," "*Baruch Hashem Adonai!*," "Bat Mitzvah!/Bar Mitzvah!," "*Ben-Yisrael!*," "*Bat-Yisrael!*," "*Kadosh L'Adonai!*."

14. For an introduction to the history and content of the Jewish Oral Law, see BEKY Booklet *Introduction to the Jewish Sources.*

- Dancing following the service. Typically, the males will dance with the bar mitzvah, and for girls, the females will dance with the bat mitzvah. Others are invited to stand back and clap, sing, wave banners, and hang onto youngsters who might wander into the celebration!
- Oneg, which is a meal celebration following the service
- Small gifts and cards for the bar mitzvah are appropriate, but excessive or large gifts should be given in the home

Although it is not traditional for adults to bar or bat mitzvah, it is becoming more and more popular for adults who were not reared in the Jewish tradition or who are Jewish and never had the bar mitzvah experience to celebrate this ancient rite of passage. It's never too late to mature in the Body of Messiah, and celebration is central to the journey of faith.

The preparation for the bar mitzvah is extensive, and it will take a year or more to prepare. Much bar mitzvah preparation requires studying with a parent, which fulfills the commandment for a parent to teach diligently the commandments to their children. Among the skills and topics learned are Biblical knowledge and structure, basic Hebrew, chanting liturgical prayers and Torah tropes [15] in Hebrew, and memorization of certain prayers and blessings. The bar mitzvah boy or bat mitzvah girl will have a Messianic understanding of the Land, People, and Scriptures of Israel, including in-depth study of covenant relationships and Yeshua's central role in the plan of redemption. Ideally, they can research rabbinical and contemporary commentaries as well as use a concordance, and they can prepare a sermon, exhortation, or commentary over the weekly Bible reading.

15. The musical notes to which the words of Scripture are sung in Hebrew.

At the end of the preparation time, the bar mitzvah will be an expert on his assigned Torah portion, which fulfills our daily prayer, "Grant us our portion in your Torah..." Along with the knowledge and skills necessary for the bar mitzvah, he must have a familiarity with the structure and order of a synagogue service.

So get ready to clap, sing, cheer, march, dance, worship, learn, and enter into the joy of the Living Torah with the bar or bat mitzvah.

7

CONCLUSION

Celebration is central to the Jewish and the Messianic worship experience. Although different from Christian worship services, Messianic worship is the root and foundation of Christian worship in spite of Christianity's later divergence from the 1st Century patterns.

Messianic congregations and fellowships are springing up worldwide, and the diversity of religious, ethnic, and academic backgrounds make every congregation interesting. Some may offer an experience similar to that of an evangelical Christian worship service, while others are little different from an Orthodox Jewish synagogue service. Learning Scripturally-founded practices in worship does not have to be intimidating, but enjoyable and fulfilling.

We hope you find your Messianic congregational visit filled with the Presence of Adonai! Although it may be different from any other service you've experienced, it is an opportunity to rest on the Sabbath in Messiah's completed work of Creation in your life.

If the prayers, song, dance, proclamation of the Word, teaching, fellowship, or any other part of the service have touched your heartstrings, let that motivate you to follow up with some additional reading.

We pray that you'll find a fulfilling fellowship near you!

FREQUENTLY ASKED QUESTIONS

Why do you turn toward the East to pray?

This is not a man-made tradition, but established by King Solomon in the inauguration of the First Temple when the Presence of Adonai was so great that the priests could not stand to minister. King Solomon knew that eventually Israel would be exiled and the Temple was destined to become a House of Prayer for all nations. He established a pattern of prayer for all who would worship the Holy One in ages to come:

Here are some excerpts from the passage in I Kings 8:

> 33..."When Your people Israel are defeated before an enemy, because they have sinned against You, if they turn to You again and confess Your name and pray and make supplication to You in this house, then hear in heaven, and forgive the sin of Your people Israel, and bring them back to the land which You gave to their fathers...

> 35 ..."When the heavens are shut up and there is no rain, because they have sinned against You, and they pray toward this place and confess Your name and turn from their sin when You afflict them, then hear in heaven and forgive the sin of Your servants and of Your people Israel, indeed, teach them

the good way in which they should walk... If there is famine in the land, if there is pestilence, if there is blight or mildew, locust or grasshopper, if their enemy besieges them in the land of their cities, whatever plague, whatever sickness there is, whatever prayer or supplication is made by any man or by all Your people Israel, each knowing the affliction of his own heart, and spreading his hands toward this house; then hear in heaven Your dwelling place, and forgive and act and render to each according to all his ways, whose heart You know...

41 ...Also concerning the foreigner who is not of Your people Israel, when he comes from a far country for Your name's sake (for they will hear of Your great name and Your mighty hand, and of Your outstretched arm); when he comes and prays toward this house, hear in heaven Your dwelling place, and do according to all for which the foreigner calls to You, in order that all the peoples of the earth may know Your name, to fear You, as do Your people Israel, and that they may know that this house which I have built is called by Your name.

Daniel is the prototype for those who live outside of Jerusalem, yet they direct their faces toward Jerusalem to pray: "He went into his house; and his windows being open in his chamber toward Jerusalem, he kneeled upon his knees three times a day, and prayed and gave thanks before his God..." (Daniel 6:10) Indeed, the Psalmist expresses the yearning thus:

If I forget you, O Jerusalem, may my right hand forget her skill. (137:5)

Some Christians unfamiliar with the custom may confuse it with Muslim prayer, or they may think of the following verse:

> And he brought me into the inner court of the LORD'S house, and, behold, at the door of the temple of the LORD, between the porch and the altar, were about five and twenty men, with their backs toward the temple of the LORD, and their faces toward the east; and they worshipped the sun toward the east. (Ezekiel 8:16)

A careful reading of Ezekiel explains that the sun-worshippers had their BACKS to the Temple. The direction of Jewish prayer is FACING the Temple.

Am I obligated to stand during the parts of the service where I would prefer not to participate?

The only seat in the Temple was the Mercy Seat. Unless you have a physical disability or illness, standing when the congregation stands is not a sign of participation in the worship, but a sign of respect for those who are worshipping (2 Kings 5:17-18). Respect is a character trait not so much in fashion in America since the 60s, but it never goes out of fashion in the Presence of Adonai. One of the Seven Spirits of Adonai listed in Isaiah is *Yirat Adonai*, or The Reverence of Adonai. Respecting those who are in the act of worshipping Him is requested.

What are those little strings the men are wearing?

Those little strings are *tzitzit*. They are to remind us of this commandment:

> The LORD also spoke to Moses, saying, 'Speak to the sons of Israel, and tell them that they shall make for themselves tassels (*tzitziyot*) on the corners of their garments throughout their generations,

and that they shall put on the tassel of each corner a cord of blue. And it shall be a tassel (*tzitzit*) for you to look at and remember all the commandments of the LORD, so as to do them and not follow after your own heart and your own eyes, after which you played the harlot, in order that you may remember to do all My commandments, and be holy to your God. I am the LORD your God who brought you out from the land of Egypt to be your God; I am the LORD your God." (Numbers 15:37-41)

Yeshua affirms the importance of keeping the commandments

If you love Me, you will keep My commandments. (John 14:15)

And Paul teaches in Romans that the commandments and Torah are spiritual (Romans 7:14), and must be kept with the strength of the resurrected spiritual man, not the man of flesh, which merely impels us to strive against the spiritual commandment and brings forth death. Our relationship with Yeshua makes our relationship to the commandments one of love, not works.

Yes, those little strings remind us of all that!

Traditionally, this commandment is fulfilled by wearing a tallit, the decorative prayer shawl, or a tallit katan, a rectangular garment concealed under or worn over the shirt. The tallit, or prayer shawl, is also used as a canopy for blessing the children or a marriage canopy under which marriage vows are taken.

There will be some diversity in when, how, or if some Messianics wear tzitzit. In a Messianic Jewish congregation, perhaps only the males wear a tallit or tallit katan. On the other hand, women may wear a suitably feminine tallit so that it cannot be confused with the male garment. In a non-Jewish Messianic congregation, you may see males or females wear them, and some may affix the tassels to their belt loops, which is not normative within Judaism. Some may wear the outer garment, a tallit, while others may conceal them as an undergarment.

Why is there so much emphasis on Hebrew?

We thought you might ask! The Torah and the Prophets for the most part were written in Hebrew. Much of the New Testament quotes those very Hebrew Scriptures. The problem with translations is that often a translation reflects the bias or cultural limitations of the translator. We can see the truth of this in the scores of English translations of the Bible.

One way to avoid having to decide on the "best" translation of a word, phrase, or verse of Scripture is to learn the language in which it was written. This eliminates the middleman and takes the individual directly to the source so he or she can respond with confidence, "It is written..."

As an example, consider the Israelites who returned from Babylon speaking other languages. When Ezra and the priests "...read from the scroll of the Teaching of God, translating it and giving the sense; so they understood the reading," the people were obtaining the Scriptures through middlemen, who were greatly used of God to explain the Hebrew Scriptures in a known tongue.

In the beginning, however, it was not so! The perfection of creation is for Adonai to walk with us in the cool of the evening speaking directly to us in a common language. Reading the Bible in Hebrew will make the Scriptures come alive and decrease dependence on human translators who may err in understanding. At the least, knowing how to use a concordance is encouraged to make personal study more profitable.

Why is the meeting so long?

In keeping the Sabbath, we trust that worshipers have set aside the obligations of the workweek to enjoy the Presence of Adonai and His children without time limitations. After all, if we were to work on Shabbat, aren't we adding to the completed work of Messiah Yeshua? It is better to delight in Yeshua's completed work of salvation! We are complete in him.

Different parts of the service minister to the needs of different people. Some love the devotion expressed in the liturgy. Some love to sing or dance. Some love the public reading of Scripture. Some need prayer for illness. Some love the teaching of the Word. Some need the fellowship of oneg. In 1 Corinthians 11, the Apostle Paul makes it clear that our coming together is not to eat alone! Adonai calls us to a congregation to teach maturity within a Body. He admonishes the Body to "wait for one another."

While not every part of the service ministers to everyone's taste, it is the patience of our Messiah to wait for others who may draw strength and spiritual or physical healing from it. My appetite may not call for some parts of the service, but they are Scriptural, and they are ministering to someone. Love is patient.

In many congregations, congregants try to provide enough food for everyone to share in the oneg meal, especially if there are visitors who have traveled a distance; this assists them in avoiding buying/selling on Shabbat:

> In those days I saw in Judah some
> who were treading wine presses on
> the sabbath, and bringing in sacks of
> grain and loading them on donkeys,
> as well as wine, grapes, figs and all
> kinds of loads, and they brought them
> into Jerusalem on the sabbath day.
> So I admonished them on the day

they sold food. Also men of Tyre were living there who imported fish and all kinds of merchandise, and sold them to the sons of Judah on the sabbath, even in Jerusalem. Then I reprimanded the nobles of Judah and said to them, "What is this evil thing you are doing, by profaning the sabbath day? "Did not your fathers do the same, so that our God brought on us and on this city all this trouble? Yet you are adding to the wrath on Israel by profaning the sabbath." It came about that just as it grew dark at the gates of Jerusalem before the sabbath, I commanded that the doors should be shut and that they should not open them until after the sabbath. Then I stationed some of my servants at the gates so that no load would enter on the sabbath day. (Nehemiah 13:15-19)

Now it came about on the sixth day they gathered twice as much bread, two omers for each one. When all the leaders of the congregation came and told Moses, then he said to them, 'This is what the LORD meant: Tomorrow is a sabbath observance, a holy sabbath to the LORD. Bake what you will bake and boil what you will boil, and all that is left over put aside to be kept until morning.' (Exodus 16:22-23)

What do all these symbols mean? And aren't some of them used in paganism?

You may see many Jewish or Biblical symbols and artwork in a Messianic fellowship. Some symbols are the menorah, the Magen David (Star of David), or even a multi-symbol with the Magen David, the cross, and a fish fused.

The best response to this question is given thoroughly in a set of DVD lectures given by Frank Houtz of Dry Bones Restoration Company, but this excerpt from a personal communication condenses his teaching concerning symbols:

"First, a star of David is a symbol. Symbols by their nature cannot have any innate meaning. They mean whatever they mean to whomever they mean it. For example, Latin letters are used in much of the European continent, in America, most of South America, Australia and even heavily throughout Africa. Even so, each letter is not pronounced the same, meaning it does not represent the same sound every time. One can assemble those letters into strings called words. Even there, the meaning of the string can be different. The pronunciation is a symbol as much as the letters. The spoken word represents a concept, but the same sounds can contain several meanings. The German word for yes is *Ja*, pronounced like *Yah*. The Hebrew word Yah is the name for God. I suspect God does not develop whiplash turning His head to hear a German, thinking the German is calling on Him with every affirmative answer. So a symbol is anything that represents another thing. It can be a sound, a letter, an emblem, an artwork, a gesture, even a poem and much, much more. It only means what the creator meant for it to mean. To suggest that a symbol will always represent a particular meaning is completely foreign to the nature of symbols.

Let's just say the symbol has the meaning that the culture assigns to it. Some superstitious people have assigned power to a certain symbol. For example, Pennsylvania Dutch would paint hex signs on their barns to ward off evil spirits. Some Roman Catholics carry images of St. Christopher to protect them during their travels. To assign power to a symbol may actually be some form of witchcraft. Isn't witchcraft the assigning power to spells, (a series of words) or amulets (a certain image or charm). If we attribute some innate power to a symbol, we are suggesting that the symbol itself can harbor evil or good and pass those attributes onto its bearer. This is a disturbing analysis of symbols.

To look for the origin of a symbol in order to establish approval or disapproval again is a misunderstanding of the nature of symbols. If a symbol had pagan origins in its history, it does not mean that it is pagan today or even would connect in anyone's mind as being pagan. Even the word pagan has changed in meaning over the years. It once meant a farmer or a peasant. Now it means an idol worshiper or polytheist. If the origin of a word supersedes the present meaning, a pagan is a good person with humble beginnings but a strong worker. The star of David may have had some use by a pagan culture, but it probably also had some use by a righteous culture. The simpler a symbol is, the more likely it has been used multiple times with multiple meanings.

I recently visited the synagogue in Capernaum, Israel. This is the synagogue where Yehoshua [16] once taught (Mark 1:21 and other verses). I found it interesting to find carved in the lintel a Magen David. It seems if this symbol were innately evil, Yehoshua would have shunned a synagogue that had this symbol on it.

I'm not sure we can conclusively prove that the Magen David is an ancient shield of David even though in the archeological digs in Israel, the Magen David was found in a mosaic on Solomon's palace floor. I'm not even certain that the symbol was always thought to be representing a star. It really doesn't look like anything I have seen in the heavens. But whether David used it or not, that does not determine its value. Truly, a sign is just that, a sign. It represents something to some group of people." (F. Houtz, personal communication, 8/6/15)

What Hebrew learning programs do you recommend?

- Easy Hebrew – www.easyhebrew.com
- Hebrew at the Speed of Light
  - www.ulpanor.com

16. Longer form of the Hebrew name Yeshua.

What books or academic articles can I read to learn more?

Books

- Barney Kasdan's *God's Appointed Times*
- Bellarmino Bagatti's (E. Hoade, Trans.)
  The Church from the Circumcision
- Brad Young's *Paul: The Jewish Theologian*
- Hal Gruber's *The Church and the Jews*
- Hollisa Alewine's *Standing With Israel*
  and *Creation Gospel Workbook Six*
- Jean Danielou's *The Theology of Jewish Christianity* (John A. Baker, Trans.)
- Leonard Elliott-Binns, *Galilean Christianity*
- ------*Primitive Christianity*
- Ray Pritz's *Nazarene Jewish Christianity:
  From the End of the New Testament Period
  Until its Disappearance in the Fourth Century*
- Richard Rives' *Too Long in the Sun*
- Ron Mosley's *Yeshua: A Guide to the
  Real Jesus and the Original Church*
- S. Creeger's *Introduction to the Jewish Sources*
- Shlomo Hizak's *The Little Sanctuary*

Articles

- Messianic Judaism: Church, Denomination,
  Sect, or Cult? By Samuelson, Francine K.
  Journal of Ecumenical Studies, Spring 2000
- Mapping Messianic Jewish Theology: A
  Constructive Approach. Contributors:
  Mayhew, Eugene J. - Author. *Journal
  of the EvangelicalT heological Society.*
  Volume: 53. Issue: 3 September 2010.
- Kinzer, M., & Juster, D. (2002). Defining
  Messianic Judaism. Retrieved May 24, 2004,
  from   http://www.umjc.org/faq/definition/
- Samuelson, F. K. (2000, Spring). Messianic
  Judaism: Church, Denomination, Sect, or
  Cult. *Journal of Ecumenical Studies*, 37(2).

QUESTIONS FOR REVIEW

1. Describe the ethnic makeup of a typical Messianic congregation:

2. Describe the Nazarenes from the First Century until 430 AD:

3. Describe a Messianic's spiritual identity and his/her view of salvation and sanctification:

4. List the typical items, such as furniture or symbols, found in a Messianic synagogue or congregation:

5. Explain the Greek word *paradosis*:

6. Contrast a "good" repetitious prayer with a "bad" one.

7. Explain the definition of prayer from the Hebrew or Jewish point of view.

8. How does prayer change the future?

9. Describe some actions that would be considered poor etiquette in a Messianic congregation:

10. Name the three types of Scripture readings typically done in a Shabbat service:

REFERENCES

Goble, P. 1996. *Everything you need to know to grow a Messianic yeshiva*. Artists for Israel International. Downloaded from http://www.afii.org/texts/eyntgamy.html 6/27/2004.

Golli, E. 1950. *The Nazarene*. (Vollert, C. Trans.). New Hope, KY: St. Martin de Porres Lay Dominican Community.

Hizak, S. (1988). *The little sanctuary*. Jerusalem: AMI – The Jerusalem Center for Biblical Studies and Research.

Houtz, F. (2010). "Discerning Between Good and Evil." (DVD). Winchester, KY: Dry Bones Restoration Company.

Kasdan, B. (1993). *God's Appointed Times*. Clarksville, MD: Messianic Jewish Resources International.

ABOUT
THE AUTHOR

Dr. Hollisa Alewine has her B.S. and M.Ed. from Texas A&M and a Doctorate from Oxford Graduate School; she is the author of Standing with Israel: A House of Prayer for All Nations, The Creation Gospel Bible study series, and a programmer on Hebraic Roots Network. Dr. Alewine is a student and teacher of the Word of God.

www.ingramcontent.com/pod-product-compliance
Lightning Source LLC
Chambersburg PA
CBHW071637040426
42452CB00009B/1664